LAKE DISTRICT
MOODS

JON SPARKS

HALSGROVE

First published in Great Britain in 2003
Reprinted 2004
Copyright © 2003 text and photographs Jon Sparks

Title page photograph: **Tree below Castle Crag**

British Library Cataloguing-in-Publication Data
A CIP record for this title is available from the British Library

ISBN 1 84114 312 X

HALSGROVE
Halsgrove House
Lower Moor Way
Tiverton, Devon EX16 6SS
Tel: 01884 243242
Fax: 01884 243325
email: sales@halsgrove.com
website: www.halsgrove.com

Printed by D'Auria Industrie Grafiche Spa, Italy

INTRODUCTION

The Lake District means many different things to many different people: the hubbub of Bowness and the silence of Little Stand; intimate woodland in Borrowdale and vast horizons on Black Combe; adrenalin-charged moments on rock-climbs like Kipling Groove and moments of quiet contemplation by Bowscale Tarn; a hasty drink from a icy spring and a leisurely pint in a cosy pub. Perhaps everyone has their own Lake District. In this book I have tried to show something of mine.

I walked the valleys and lower fells on family holidays from a very early age and in due course, moved on to the higher tops. Scrambling and climbing, both on rock and ice, just seemed like a natural progression. Recently I have been discovering, or rediscovering, many of the tracks on a mountain bike.

The Lake District is a great place to pursue all of these activities, and each has shown me new facets. Each in its own way brings you closer to the fabric and texture of the place. Climbing, for instance, instils an acute awareness of the fine detail of rock. And, whatever I have been doing in the Lakes, since my teenage years I have invariably carried a camera. Photography, too, has helped me to look at things in different ways: to look at rock in terms of form and pattern and colour as well as holds and belays.

It is really quite a small area. A fit person can walk across it in a day. But the more you explore, the bigger it seems to get. I have been discovering the Lakes for over thirty years and still there are new paths to walk, crags to climb, tracks to ride. At the same time, there are places I can go to again and again, sure that I will see something new each time. The turn of the seasons, the shift of the light, the ever-changing weather, sees to that.

Some people grumble about the Lake District weather. But the weather is one of the things that makes it so endlessly interesting. There are days of crystal clarity and days when everything is wreathed in shifting mist; days of hard frost and – just occasionally – days when it is almost too hot to walk. Sometimes you can get virtually every kind of weather in a single day. For the photographer this means, above all, that the light is constantly changing. Would I like to live somewhere where the sun always shines? Not in a million years.

I have been exploring the district for many years, and plan to go on doing so as long as I can still walk. This book is not the last word; just the story so far.

Jon Sparks

LAKE DISTRICT NATIONAL PARK

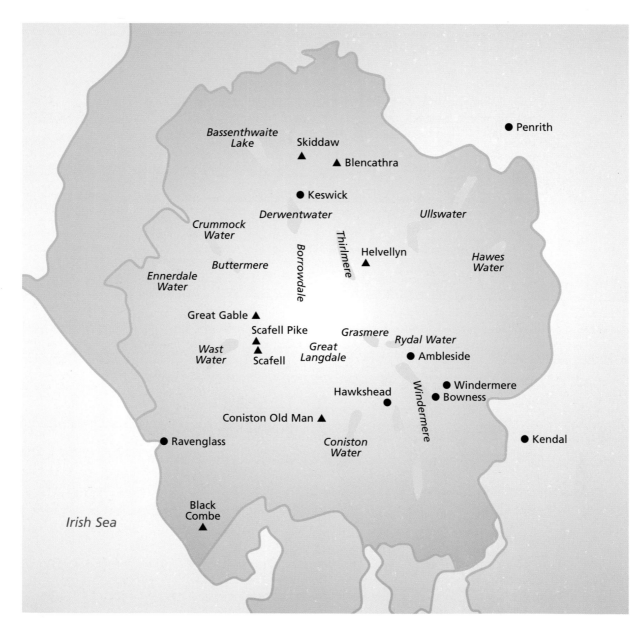

Penrith

Bassenthwaite Lake

Skiddaw ▲

▲ Blencathra

● Keswick

Derwentwater

Ullswater

Crummock Water

Thirlmere

Borrowdale

Helvellyn ▲

Buttermere

Hawes Water

Ennerdale Water

Great Gable ▲

Scafell Pike
▲
▲
Scafell

Grasmere

Rydal Water

Wast Water

Great Langdale

● Ambleside

Hawkshead
●

Windermere

● Windermere
● Bowness

Coniston Old Man ▲

● Ravenglass

Coniston Water

● Kendal

Black Combe
▲

Irish Sea

Crummock Water from Low Fell
*Low Fell is a short climb, though a steep one, but the effort is rewarded with one of the finest of
Lake District panoramas.   Beyond Crummock Water, Buttermere can also be glimpsed and beyond,
on the horizon, is Great Gable.   Nearer and to the right, overlooking the lakes, is the High Stile
range and, closer to the camera, Mellbreak.*

Coniston panorama

Coniston Water makes a fine mirror for the sunlit fells. Dow Crag is on the left, with Coniston Old Man to its right. Swirl How is half-hidden by the Old Man and further right again is the double hump of Wetherlam. On the far right, clouds partly cover the Fairfield Horseshoe.

Meadowsweet and wall, near Sandwick
Meadowsweet – a member of the rose family – runs riot in these fields near Sandwick,
on the south-eastern shore of Ullswater.

Walls, Wasdale Head
*The thickness of these walls, and the extra heaps of stone, suggests the sheer
hard labour that was necessary to clear the ground for these pastures.*

Summit of Eel Crag
Eel Crag, also known as Crag Hill, is one of the principal summits in the north-western fells. On this superb winter's day, the Pennines stand out clearly in the distance. To the left is the distinctive shape of Blencathra and, to the right, the long, easy ridges of the Dodds. Closer again lie the town of Keswick and a section of Derwentwater and, just to its right, the knobbly ridge of Causey Pike.

Sour Milk Gill, Borrowdale
Some names recur repeatedly through the Lakes; there are numerous Eagle Crags and Raven Crags, for instance, and there are three well-known Sour Milk Gills. This is a detail of the one that runs down to Seathwaite in Borrowdale.

Wall above Raven Crag
Of the many Raven Crags, this is the one in Combe Gill, Borrowdale. The wall was built to prevent sheep straying onto the steep rocks. A little of Borrowdale can be seen below, with Skiddaw on the horizon.

Rocks near Birks Bridge
Birks Bridge, in the upper Duddon valley, is a popular spot, but it wasn't the bridge itself that attracted me so much as these water-worn rocks just a few metres upstream.

Grass and wall, Claife Heights
*On the way down to Near Sawrey from Claife Heights, my eye was caught by the
delicate shapes of these sunlit grasses against a shadowed drystone wall, with
some meadow buttercups for extra colour.*

Lichen, Borrowdale
This rock was so covered in lichen that the colour of the stone itself was almost completely masked.
There are several species here, but the yellow splotches of map lichen dominate.

Stickle Tarn and Pavey Ark

On busy days, hundreds of walkers make the steep climb from Great Langdale to Stickle Tarn. Some go no further, but most continue to the summit of Pavey Ark. There are easy routes which avoid the crags entirely, but perhaps the most popular way is by Jack's Rake, which scrambles up the face diagonally from lower right to upper left. There are also many rock-climbs on this massive crag.

Bracken Gill and the slopes of Lingmell
*The bulk of Lingmell, a subsidiary
of Scafell Pike, keeps the sun from the
fields of Wasdale Head for much of the
morning, and it was early afternoon before
the raking light revealed the details of the
fell itself. At the base of Bracken Gill
is a fan of debris washed down from
above, now largely stabilised and
covered, appropriately, with bracken.*

Trees by the River Derwent, Borrowdale
The woods of lower Borrowdale are a rich mixture of species; these are common alder, which often grows by water and is exceptionally tolerant of occasional immersion. The shady, humid conditions and clean air also favour the growth of lichen.

Barn and moon, Borrans Field
This fine example of a Lake District barn is found at Borrans Field, near Ambleside. The upper floor would typically be a hayloft while animals would be housed below. Such barns were normally built into a slope, allowing 'ground-level' access to both floors.

Sheep, tree and Wetherlam
The viewpoint is just below Latterbarrow, not far from Hawkshead. In the distance is Wetherlam, occupying the north-eastern corner of the Coniston fells.

Side House, Great Langdale
Evening light shining across the slopes of Lingmoor Fell helps to bring out the texture of the landscape.
The green pastures of the valley floor contrast with the rougher enclosures of the lower slopes and
the extensive stands of bracken, gorse and juniper above.

Rainbows, near Kendal
*Sunshine and a shower, in early autumn, produced these vivid rainbows, seen from the slopes of
Cunswick Scar, looking across the valley of the River Kent.*

The River Brathay near Elter Water
Extensive reed beds surround the shallow tarn of Elter Water and also line the River Brathay which flows from it.
Among the reeds are the tall pinkish spikes of purple-loosestrife.

Ennerdale from Brin Crag

Getting slightly lost can be highly rewarding. Having wandered off the main track to Great Gable, I stumbled across this fine viewpoint. The craggy north face of Pillar looms over the valley while Red Pike appears over Black Sail Pass. Further right is the tangled top of Haystacks, with High Crag and High Stile beyond.

The River Duddon, below Duddon Bridge

The Duddon valley was a great favourite of Wordsworth and he wrote a series of sonnets about it, one of which includes the well-known line, 'Still glides the stream, and shall for ever glide.' Whichever sense of the word 'still' you choose, it seems to fit this placid stretch in the lower reaches of the river.

Moss, Lodore
*A macro lens was required for this shot,
taken close to the well-known falls at
Lodore in Borrowdale: this miniature forest
is really only a few centimetres high.*

Rowan, Launchy Gill
Launchy Gill runs steeply down through the forest on the west side of Thirlmere, and some of its cascades can be seen from a nature trail. The rowan (also known misleadingly as mountain ash) does not really like shady places, and this tree is probably a survivor from before the establishment of the conifer plantations.

Opposite: Gable Beck
This fine waterfall is not particularly well-known; only walkers approaching (or descending from) Great Gable by the steep direct route known as Gavel Neese are likely to see it. The summit of Gable is hidden but the steep crags of the Napes show up well.

Sheep, above the Duddon valley
This shot was taken late on a summer evening, high on the ridge of Brown Pike, looking down to the fields of the Duddon valley. The sheep on the right is probably the mother of the one on the left: adults are shorn in early summer.

Cascades, River Caldew
The River Caldew, which rises on the slopes of Skiddaw, cuts a deep valley through the northern fells. Below Bowscale Fell is a fine series of cascades of which this is just a part. The slopes of Coomb Height, beyond, are typical of the bare rounded hills which lie 'Back o'Skiddaw'.

Ice, Easedale
After a few days' hard frost, the splashes from a tiny beck had built up into these intricate ice formations, most of which were built on a core of a grass or rush stem.

Coniston Water and the Coniston fells from Brock Barrow
Brock Barrow is the abrupt southern end of the broad moorland which lies east of Coniston Water.
From the summit cairn there is an unequalled view of the lake. The central, and highest, peak is Coniston
Old Man. To its left is Dow Crag, to its right Swirl How and the two tops of Wetherlam.

Beck and wall, Loughrigg Terrace
Loughrigg Terrace, above Grasmere, is a very popular walk. One day, after heavy rain, this mini-waterfall appeared when the usual channel became blocked with debris.

A mixture of ferns, Borrowdale
Ferns generally prefer moist shady places, and there are plenty of those in Borrowdale. The main species here, especially on the right of the picture, is hard fern, with beech fern on its left.

Rocks, Coniston

*The Coniston fells are one of the most mineral-rich areas of the Lake District,
and are particularly associated with the mining of copper. The beautiful colouring of
these rocks on the slopes of Coniston Old Man is due to a mix of minerals, including
chalcopyrite, which was the main copper ore.*

Opposite: **Goldrill Beck and Brothers Water**

*Brothers Water – often written as one word – lies near the head of the Patterdale valley and the
popular track to Dovedale runs close to its western shore. This shot is looking south from the
outlet of the lake, where it feeds Goldrill Beck. Kirkstone Pass is the obvious 'V' on the skyline.*

Sunbeams, High Raise
The weather in the Lakes is notoriously changeable, and even the least promising day can yield moments like this. The summit of Bowfell is just discernible through the sunbeams but to its right Esk Pike and Great End are still covered by cloud.

Ennerdale, evening
After a day's climbing on Gable Crag, we made our way back towards Honister Pass along the old track known as Moses' Trod. The sun was sinking behind Kirk Fell and the fells further west – Pillar left of centre, High Stile further right – hardly seemed solid at all.

Winter light, Ludderburn
A few miles south of Bowness-on-Windermere is this small area of pools and reed-beds, skirted by a relatively new permissive path. It is always fascinating, but the low light of a winter day made it especially beautiful.

Sculpted snow, Helvellyn

Descending from Helvellyn at the end of a winter's day, we passed these examples of natural sculpture: snow shaped simply by sun and wind. Crinkle Crags and Bowfell can be seen on the horizon.

Ice, Derwentwater
Did the water level drop to strand these plates of ice, or were they pushed to shore by the breeze? Probably a little of both. On the skyline are two of the district's most popular fells: Catbells, near the centre of the shot, and Causey Pike on the right.

Frosty morning at High Dam
High Dam, near the southern end of Windermere, rivals the better-known Tarn Hows. Certainly you are much more likely to have the place to yourself here, especially on a chilly morning like this.

Herdwick in snow
Some would say that Beatrix Potter's greatest legacy, at least as far as the Lake District is concerned, is her role in preserving the Herdwick sheep. This hardy breed produces tough, vari-coloured wool and finely-flavoured meat.

Opposite: **Sunrise, near Hawkshead Hill**
The bare branches of this oak tree seem to glow in the light of the rising sun on a fine cold morning in early January.

Summit of Pike o'Stickle
*Pike o'Stickle is the westernmost top
of the Langdale Pikes. The conical summit
(left) is Loft Crag, with the clean rock face of
Gimmer Crag below to its right. Blea Tarn
is near the centre of the picture and
Windermere is directly behind Loft Crag.
Esthwaite Water is further right and
Morecambe Bay appears in the distance.*

Woods, from Black Crag

Black Crag lies in the little side valley of Troutdale and here we are looking over the intervening ridge to the main Borrowdale valley; part of the village of Grange can be seen. It will surprise many people to realise that these woods are not ancient; paintings from the eighteenth and nineteenth centuries show a much more open landscape.

Windsurfer, Coniston Water
The light of a summer evening catches the bright sail of a windsurfer in splendid isolation on Coniston Water.
The summit behind is Black Sails, the lower western top of Wetherlam.

Cathedral Quarry
There are few natural caves in the Lake District, but quarrying has created a number of spectacular artificial ones.
This one is in one of the old quarries of Tilberthwaite, between Little Langdale and Coniston. It is easily entered
by a level tunnel and thanks to the large 'window' torches are not needed.

Misty morning, Rydal Water
*Heron Island, the larger of two islands in Rydal Water, stands out solidly against
the sketchy outlines of Loughrigg Fell behind.*

Grasmere

Grasmere, though about twice the size of neighbouring Rydal Water, is still one of the smallest of the recognised lakes. In this picture, looking north from near the outflow, the deep notch in the skyline is Dunmail Raise, the main route between the northern and southern parts of the district.

Boulder, south ridge of Esk Pike

The long south ridge of Esk Pike, remote and little-trodden, overlooks one of the wildest parts of the district. Across upper Eskdale are the highest peaks in the Lake District: on the left Scafell and in the centre of the picture Scafell Pike. Right again are Broad Crag and Ill Crag. Directly below Scafell Pike is Esk Buttress, one of the finest climbing crags in England.

Dow Crag from Goat's Water
Dow Crag is both one of the best and one of the most accessible of the high mountain crags of the Lake District, and the worn tracks up the screes are evidence of its enduring popularity. There are routes for experienced scramblers as well as rock climbs of all grades.

Parsley Fern
The fronds of parsley fern certainly resemble the leaves of parsley, but it is a fern, not a herb.
Despite its delicate appearance, it is a tough plant, typically found on high crags and screes.

Burning leaves, Winster
*Sunbeams filter through the smoke from
burning leaves under the beech trees in the
churchyard at Winster.*

Grasmere and Helm Crag
A misty morning on Grasmere. The prominent fell on the left is Silver How, while the shadowed hill on the right is Helm Crag, sometimes known as the Lion and the Lamb after the appearance (from a certain angle) of its summit rocks.

Great Gable from Broad Crag

*Great Gable is one of the best-known and best-loved of the fells. Its outline forms part of the emblem
of the National Park. The Napes crags were the scene of some of the earliest development in rock-climbing,
and its summit is the site of the Fell and Rock Climbing Club's War Memorial. A Remembrance Day
service still takes place there every year, whatever the weather.*

Red Tarn, snow
Red Tarn lies below Helvellyn, between the aretes of Striding Edge, on the left, and Swirral Edge, on the right. Winter or summer, on any fine day, dozens and often hundreds of walkers traverse the ridges.

Walkers, below Castle Crag
Castle Crag rises steeply above the River Derwent, forming one side of the 'Jaws of Borrowdale'. This shot is looking down to the south-west, on a track which makes a pleasant route for walkers and cyclists between Seatoller and Grange.

Larches, Hill Fell
*The larch is a conifer, but not an evergreen;
its needles turn gold in autumn before they
fall. But it was the rays of the setting sun
that made them appear almost to be on fire.
This is on Hill Fell, between Hawkshead
Hill and Tarn Hows.*

Opposite: Oak roots, Glencoyne
*I set out to photograph the wild daffodils
at Glencoyne, on the shores of Ullswater,
where they inspired the famous poem
by Wordsworth, but found myself much
more attracted by the tangle of roots
of this great oak tree.*

Bell heather, Gummer's How
*Two species of heather are found in the Lake
District: 'ordinary' heather, also known as
ling, and bell heather.*

Opposite: **Rock detail, by the River Caldew**
*These water-worn rocks were still clean in
places, suggesting that the river still washes
over them when it is running high.*

Cormorant, Windermere

Only this cormorant taking off – its track reminiscent of skimming stones – disturbed the surface of Windermere early on an autumn morning.

Reindeer moss and heather, Ullscarf
Ullscarf is a sprawling fell on the central ridge of the district, between Thirlmere and Borrowdale.
It is often disparaged as a boring lump, but if you keep your eyes open there is plenty to see, like this fine
garden: not just reindeer moss (actually a lichen) and heather, but ferns, rushes, grasses and bilberry.

Laid tree, below Whitbarrow

The strange shape of this hawthorn shows that it was once part of a 'laid' hedge. The laying of hedges involves cutting the stems part-way through to allow them to be laid almost horizontally, forming an effective stock barrier. It is a labour-intensive business and it's little wonder that many of these hedges have fallen into neglect or been replaced with post-and-wire.

Windermere, clearing mist
Early on a November morning, clearing mists reveal the distinctive outlines of Crinkle Crags, Bowfell and the Langdale Pikes.

Scafell Pinnacle

*Scafell Pinnacle is one of a small number of Lakeland summits which cannot be reached by walkers –
even the easiest route, on the short side, is a rock climb. The long side gives climbs up to 100 metres (328ft) in length.
However, there is a walkers' route on Scafell Crag, via Lord's Rake and the West Wall Traverse, parts of which can
be seen below, and the upper reaches of the gully which is known as Deep Gill.*

Beech leaves in pool, by Tarn Hows
*It definitely pays to look down at your feet from time to time. These freshly-fallen leaves
in their shallow pool provided an intense concentration of autumnal colour.*

Polypody ferns on wall, near Torver
Polypody fern is common on walls and trees over much of the district. Orange-coloured spore-cases cover the backs of the leaves.

Frost crystals, Gowbarrow Fell

When I spotted these frost crystals in a slight hollow on the ridge of Gowbarrow Fell, I knew I had to work quickly but carefully. The sun would melt them rapidly, but a dropped lens cap or a clumsy move with the tripod would shatter their delicacy even more decisively. I came back past this spot less than half an hour later and the frost had all gone.

Helvellyn from Ill Bell
*This was a magical mid-winter day; clear and calm and we had the fells almost to ourselves.
Helvellyn is the highest peak, near the centre of the skyline. Closer, across the upper reaches of the
Troutbeck valley, is Caudale Moor. Blencathra appears to its right.*

Looking north from Hampsfell
*All the limestone ridges around the south-eastern boundary of the National Park provide
excellent walking, and great views. The fertile Vale of Cartmel fills the middle distance; the Coniston Fells,
Langdale Pikes and Helvellyn form the skyline.*

Elterwater from Dow Bank
*Parts of both the village (Elterwater) and the lake (Elter Water) can be seen.
The mists gradually cleared, but the frost persisted all day.*

Pool on Whiteless Pike
*Concentric rings in the ice show how the pool must have frozen in stages over
several days without disturbance from wind, walkers or sheep.*

Gillercombe
*Most people would agree that bogs like this are best observed from a distance; certainly this view,
from high on Gillercombe Buttress, revealed patterns that would not be seen from ground level.
This is one of the best examples in the district of a glaciated hanging valley.*

Trees below Black Crag
After climbing Troutdale Pinnacle on Black Crag, I noticed the almost translucent spring foliage of these trees just below. They're mostly birch, though there are one or two young oaks as well. Behind it is possible to make out the outline of Maiden Moor.

Woodland detail, Torver
*The skeletons of last year's leaves give away the scale of this miniature landscape.
I wasn't just on my knees to get this photograph, but right down on my stomach,
with the camera and macro lens at ground level.*

Opposite: **Packhorse bridge, Wasdale Head**
*This old bridge is always an attractive structure, but what really caught my
eye was the reflected light on its underside.*

Summit of Stybarrow Dodd

*The wind which had formed the hoar-frost on the summit cairn was still blowing and it was bitterly cold even in the sun.
The snowfall had been localised: a mere dusting outlined the ridge running north to Watson's Dodd and Great Dodd
and there was scarcely any on the higher peaks of Skiddaw and Blencathra.*

Cascade, Cove Quarry
Cove Quarry, on the side of Coniston Old Man, has a number of artificial caves. I stood just inside the entrance of one to photograph the veil of water running over the mouth of the tunnel: much of it came from melting snow on the slope above.

Fossils, Coniston

The Coniston Limestone forms a narrow belt of rocks which make no great impact on the larger landscape, but I did find these fossil shells right by the popular Walna Scar track. I have been past many times since and never spotted them again: I don't know whether they have been purloined by a geological collector or I just haven't looked hard enough.

Great Langdale from Swinescar Pike
Even under these conditions, the sinuous curve of Great Langdale and the craggy outline of the Langdale Pikes are instantly recognisable. Pike o'Blisco is just clear of the clouds on the left but at the head of the valley Crinkle Crags and Bowfell are obscured.

Striding Edge in winter
Days like this, with fresh snow, no wind, and fantastic visibility, do not occur every winter. It's no wonder there was a steady stream of walkers making their way along Striding Edge On the summit we also encountered several skiers and a couple of hardy mountain-bikers.

Opposite: **Reeds, Coniston Water**
Reed-beds are found along the shores of many of the lakes and tarns; on Coniston Water they are mostly around the southern end of the lake.

Delta, Derwentwater
*The delta where the River Derwent flows into Derwentwater is by far the most striking in the district.
Its shape is best appreciated from above.*

Wastwater Screes, evening
There are screes at many places in the Lake District, but The Screes invariably means those above Wastwater, which stretch almost the full length of the lake. There is a popular, though very rough, path traversing the base of the screes which can just be seen in the photograph.

Larches, Grizedale Forest
*It was the repetitive shapes, along with the fine light, that drew my eye to these larches;
they are very alike, but never exactly the same.*

Walker at Coledale Hause
*A light fall of snow was almost lost among the rough grass, so that only on the bare paths
did it appear to cover the ground.*

Ullswater from Gowbarrow Fell

A mixture of smoke and mist hangs over the villages of Glenridding and Patterdale. The lowest point on the skyline is Grisedale Hause; to its left is St Sunday Crag, with Fairfield partly hidden behind. To its right are Dollywaggon Pike, Nethermost Pike and Helvellyn.

Opposite: **Grasmoor from Hause Point**

Hause Point, on the shore of Crummock Water, is a good place from which to appreciate the sheer bulk of Grasmoor, highest of the north-western fells.

Deer, near Graythwaite
I originally set up the camera just to photograph the sunbeams through the trees.
When two deer took up positions exactly where I would have asked them, it seemed almost
too good to be true. The third one was slightly less obliging, but I shouldn't complain.

Daffodils and wall, Winster valley
Everyone photographs the 'Wordsworth' daffodils at Glencoyne, but they appear all over the district. I particularly liked the contrast of their freshness against the dead bracken stems and the solidity of the wall behind.

Frosty morning, Coniston Water
*A frosty February morning on the eastern shore of Coniston Water,
looking across to Dow Crag and Coniston Old Man.*

Bowfell from Wansfell
Hazy days can be frustrating for landscape photography – until the sun sinks low. Then, especially when you are looking towards the light, everything begins to glow and solid hills can seem almost translucent.

The Duddon Estuary and Black Combe from Caw
The estuary is that of the Duddon, but the sunlit valley in the middle distance is that of its
tributary, the Lickle. Black Combe – on the right – is, like Caw, overlooked by many walkers
but both are rewarding climbs and exceptional viewpoints.

Starry Saxifrage, White Gill
The starry saxifrage is a widespread and typical flower of the high fells. Here it grows in the boulder-strewn bed of White Gill, above Great Langdale.

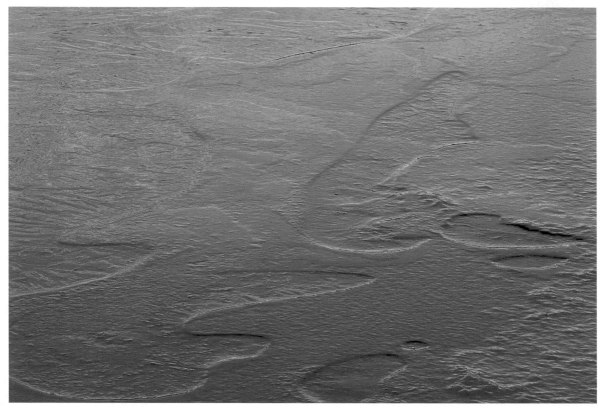

Ice, Greenburn

Greenburn Beck, above Little Langdale, forms a series of small pools in a level part of its valley.
I was intrigued by the forms of the ice and the colours reflected from sunlit fellsides and blue sky.

Frozen Tarn, Little Stand
Many people climb Crinkle Crags each year, but few of them do so by way of its south ridge.
This has a distinct intermediate summit called Little Stand and this tiny tarn is just below it.
The hill in the background is Scafell.

Eel Crags and Dale Head
These particular Eel Crags are on the side of High Spy, whose distinctive summit cairn is on the skyline.
Across the head of Newlands valley is the steep north face of Dale Head.

Upper Eskdale from Border End

Hardknott Pass is far better known than Hard Knott, the fell from which it gets its name.
Border End is a shoulder of Hard Knott and even closer to the pass. Its view of upper
Eskdale can be dramatic even on a cloudy day. Scafell and Scafell Pike are hidden, but
Esk Pike just ducks under the clouds.

Beech leaves, near Tarn Hows
Beech is not really part of the natural woodland community, but has been widely-planted and subsequently naturalised, as in the semi-artificial landscape around Tarn Hows. The tarn itself is also artificial, having been formed by damming; previously there were three much smaller tarns here. This has not stopped it becoming one of the best-loved spots in the district.

Limestone pavement, Whitbarrow

*Whitbarrow is the grandest of the limestone ridges in the south-eastern corner of the district, its full length
giving a fine walk of about 5km (3 miles). The summit, called Lord's Seat, is seen on the skyline.
Much of the area around it is now a nature reserve.*

Sheep near Ashness Bridge

*Ashness Bridge is something of a honey-pot; perhaps these sheep had chosen to shelter in this spot,
just by the car-park, in the hope of a few handouts from the tourists.*

River Rothay, White Moss
The Rothay links Grasmere and Rydal Water and subsequently flows on into Windermere. White Moss is a very popular spot, both in its own right and as a starting point for a walk onto Loughrigg Fell.

Troutbeck Park and the Ill Bell Ridge
The farmstead of Troutbeck Park lies at the foot of The Tongue, which splits the Troutbeck valley.
The Trout Beck itself runs on the west (near) side. The gap in the skyline is Threshthwaite Mouth,
and the peaks to its right are Thornthwaite Crag, Froswick and Ill Bell.

Cotton-grass, near Bell Crags
*Bell Crags is a fine rocky summit close to the Thirlmere-Watendlath track. Cotton-grass, also
known as bog cotton, is a characteristic plant of upland bogs and a useful indicator of places
where it is probably too wet to walk.*

Blackthorn, Whitbarrow
Blackthorn is a member of the cherry family and like many of its relatives produces a mass of flowers in early spring, before the leaves have appeared. Unlike most of its relatives, however, it is very spiny and has often been used to create an impenetrable barrier to livestock.

The Langdale Pikes from Loughrigg Tarn

There's no avoiding the Langdale Pikes; their distinctive outline appears in any number of views. This one, from Loughrigg Tarn, is one of the best. Loft Crag and the more distant Pike o'Stickle appear as twin summits. The deep ravine of Dungeon Ghyll separates them from Harrison Stickle, the highest of the Pikes, and Pavey Ark.

Morecambe Bay from Lad Crag
*Lad Crag is a shoulder of Helvellyn. This view looks across Nethermost Pike and Great Rigg towards
the distant Morecambe Bay, with the Forest of Bowland on the skyline.*

Castlerigg Stone Circle and the Dodds
Of the many stone circles in the British Isles, Castlerigg occupies one of the most dramatic sites.
Early morning and evening are the best times to appreciate it, not only because the light is at its best,
but because you have more chance of having the stones to yourself. We will never know for sure
why Neolithic people built these monuments, but it is fascinating to speculate.

Scafell Pike from Ill Crag
*Ill Crag is itself over 915 metres (3000 feet) but usually considered to be merely a subsidiary top
of Scafell Pike, England's highest mountain. However, its summit, a little way off the direct route
to the Pike, is usually much quieter than its famous neighbour.*

The Coniston Fells from Watson's Dodd
Apart from Dow Crag, all the main Coniston summits are visible in this picture:
Wetherlam, Coniston Old Man, Swirl How, and Grey Friar.

Waterhead from Todd Crag
Todd Crag, a shoulder of Loughrigg Fell, looks steeply down on the northern end of Windermere. The long valley of England's largest lake often holds mist when everywhere else is clear: I watched this lake cruise launch leave Waterhead Pier in sunshine but it was soon swallowed up by the fog.

Windermere from Robin Lane
*Robin Lane is a pleasant track which gives the start of a fine walk from Troutbeck to Ambleside.
It is one of the best places for studying the full length of Windermere, though from here it almost
looks like two separate lakes. Belle Isle, off Bowness, nearly cuts it in two.*

Dock Tarn
Dock Tarn lies on Great Crag, above the Stonethwaite valley. It can also be easily reached from Watendlath.
A good time to visit is late summer, when the water-lilies, after which is was named, are in flower.

Insects, Wain Lane
I liked the way these insects caught the light against a shadowy background. But what were they?
Flying ants? They moved away before I could get close enough to tell.

Pool by Tarn Hows
Steady rain kept the crowds away from Tarn Hows, but this helped to create a peaceful and intimate atmosphere.

Knapweed, Measand Beck
*Measand Beck flows into Haweswater
and its falls – named The Forces – are
fairly well-known, though far less-visited
than over-rated attractions like Aira
Force and Lodore Falls.*

The Duddon valley from Thwaites Fell

From the 'Fell Road', which cuts across the ridge north of Black Combe, there is this fine view towards the heart of the district. The snowy hill on the left is Scafell and Esk Pike, Bowfell and Crinkle Crags are also dusted in white, as are the nearer Coniston Fells.

Winter evening, Birkhouse Moor
Higher up, as it runs out of the picture on the right, this ridge becomes the celebrated Striding Edge.
The last rays of the sun strike the rocky flanks of St Sunday Crag. Beyond is the broad mass of
Fairfield and the deep notch of Grisedale Hause.

The Coniston Fells from Ill Bell
A layer of cloud creates a murky atmosphere over the intervening lowlands, but the summits are bathed in sunshine:
the principal tops here are Coniston Old Man, Wetherlam and Swirl How, the latter two almost in line.

Bistort, Troutbeck
Bistort is a common wayside plant in the district. Its tender leaves were traditionally gathered as an ingredient for a herb-pudding known as Easter-ledges.

Foxgloves and boulder, Great Langdale
Foxgloves grow well on disturbed ground and are often seen on the screes below the crags.

Opposite: **Blencathra from Tewet Tarn**
*Evening light still warms the heights of Blencathra, contrasting with
the cold sky-light over Tewet Tarn.*

Woods, Winster valley
Though close to the bustle of Bowness, the Winster valley is a good place to escape from the crowds.

Larch and Helvellyn
*These trees stand above the little valley of Whit Beck, close to
the main path up Skiddaw. Helvellyn is in the background.*

Sharp Edge, Blencathra
Sharp Edge, like Striding Edge, is one of those places where fell-walking gets a little closer to mountaineering.
The broad slopes beyond belong to Bowscale Fell and Bannerdale Crags; the distant Eden valley is almost lost in haze.

Falling snow, Lyth valley
An approaching snow shower advances across the Lyth valley, seen here from Scout Scar, near Kendal.

Evening on Grey Knotts
An early spring evening on Grey Knotts. Remnants of snow linger on the high fells. Scafell Pike is the highest peak, on the right. Great End is in the centre and Esk Pike and Bowfell further left.

Reeds, Brotherswater
*Winter gales and floods had left every stem bent or broken,
but the patterns they made still appealed.*

Walker, Gasgale Gill
Late afternoon sunlight picks out the repeating ridges and gullies of Gasgale Crags, below the peak of Whiteside.

Opposite: **Buttermere, High Crag and High Stile**
This is one of several classic views which can be enjoyed by anyone who undertakes the easy walk around Buttermere.

Reflections, Goldrill Beck

Simply the reflection of some leafless trees. What was intriguing was finding the right angle, so that the bed of the stream could be seen without distracting attention from the patterns. As they were constantly changing, I shot several frames, and this was the one I liked best.

Ill Crag and Esk Pike
As we paused near the summit of Scafell Pike, Esk Pike was briefly bathed in sunlight while nearer Ill Crag remained in shadow. The prominent knob on the next ridge is Sergeant Man and the highest of the distant, hazy ridges is High Street.

Esthwaite Water, morning
Calm conditions are most likely to be found in the early morning – whether it's the absence of wind or the absence of people that you are looking for.

Falling snow, from Eel Crag

On a day where wintry showers alternated with moments of bright sunshine, I got this shot looking down the valley of Sail Beck, with the High Stile ridge beyond. This was the trailing edge of one of the showers; the snow was only falling in a narrow band close to the camera.

Cornice, Helvellyn
This wind-shaped snow assumes many of the forms associated with sand dunes.
Part of Striding Edge can be seen on the right, with the Pennines beyond.

Low tide, Ravenglass

The Lake District National Park only reaches the coast in a few places. These include the Leven and Kent estuaries on Morecambe Bay, and a stretch of the Irish Sea coast between Silecroft and Ravenglass. At Ravenglass, the Rivers Irt and Esk meet in a complicated estuary, shielded by impressive dunes.

Stitchwort, near Hawkshead
Stitchwort is typically a hedgerow plant and doesn't often form quite such a solid mass.

Newlands valley from Causey Pike
*The clouds were moving rapidly
and so, in consequence, were the
occasional shafts of sunlight.*

Gooseyfoot Tarn
The tarn is tucked away in the northern part of Grizedale Forest. Well-used forest tracks run nearby on two sides but it seems most walkers pass without realising it's there. Like many of the tarns in the lower fells, it is at least partly artificial.

The Scafell range and Great Gable from High Spy
Great Gable appears to be the highest thing in sight, but only because it is nearer.
Scafell Pike is the snowy mass left of centre, with Scafell Crag to its right.

Evening mists, from Moses' Trod
Mist spilling from the Buttermere valley into Ennerdale is coloured by the rays of the setting sun.
Perhaps it needs to be stressed that no filters were used; this is a fair representation of what I saw.

Evening, Bassenthwaite Lake
*Bassenthwaite Lake is in fact the only lake in the Lake District. All the others are 'meres' or 'waters'.
(Phrases like 'Lake Windermere' are nonsensical.) In the distance, the moon rises over the Helvellyn range.*

Climbers on Kern Knotts
Kern Knotts is a small crag on the slopes of Great Gable, which has attracted climbers since the earliest days of the sport. Here, the leading climber is setting out on Innominate Crack, first climbed in 1921. Below are Wasdale Head and Yewbarrow, with just a small section of Wastwater visible, and the Irish Sea beyond.